Peer Pressure

Gail B. Stewart

KIDHAVEN
PRESS™

THOMSON

™

GALE

San Diego • Detroit • New York • San Francisco • Cleveland
New Haven, Conn. • Waterville, Maine • London • Munich

© 2003 by KidHaven Press. KidHaven Press is an imprint of The Gale Group, Inc., a division of Thomson Learning, Inc.

KidHaven™ and Thomson Learning™ are trademarks used herein under license.

For more information, contact
KidHaven Press
27500 Drake Rd.
Farmington Hills, MI 48331-3535
Or you can visit our Internet site at http://www.gale.com

LIBRARY OF CONGRESS CATALOGING-IN-PUBLICATION DATA

Stewart, Gail B., 1949–
  Peer pressure / by Gail B. Stewart.
    v. cm. — (Understanding issues)
  Includes bibliographical references and index.
  Summary: The power of the peer group — The growing importance of peers — A closer look at peer pressure — Being an individual.
    ISBN 0-7377-1024-1 (hardback : alk. paper)
    1. Peer pressure—Juvenile literature. [1. Peer pressure.] I. Title. II. Series.
  HQ784.P43 S74 2003
  303.3'27—dc21

                           2002012558

Printed in the United States of America

Contents

Chapter One

The Power of the Peer Group

Marny was eleven when she did something she was later ashamed of.

"I was with two of my friends," she says. "They had come to my house for a sleepover. My parents were upstairs watching television. Sarah, Julie, and I were downstairs. We were bored, and Sarah suggested calling some boys."

They tried calling two boys they liked, but no one was home. Then Sarah had an idea. They would call Sam.

Calling Sam

"Sam was a boy in our grade, but he had no friends," Marny remembers. "He was fat and kind of sloppy. He wasn't good in sports. He seemed to be alone all the time. Maybe every class has a boy like Sam—someone who just can't fit in. Some of the kids made fun of him, I guess.

"Sarah and Julie wanted to play a trick on him. They wanted to pretend they liked him. Sarah said it would be fun. At first I said I didn't think it was a good idea. I told them we might get caught. Really, it wasn't that. I just didn't feel like it was right. But they were set on it, and I wasn't brave enough to argue. I said okay, I'd go along. We all agreed we would take a turn talking to Sam.

"So we called him. Sarah asked him if he had a girl-friend. Sam said no, he didn't. She told him all the girls had a crush on him. I talked, too—I told him we all thought he was the cutest boy in the class."

People act differently around friends than when they are alone.

"It Was So Mean"

Marny shook her head while remembering that night. "It was so mean. He believed us. He thought we were being nice to him. But we weren't. We were making fun of him. We were trying hard not to laugh. After we got off the phone, Sarah and Julie kept laughing. They wanted to call all our friends and tell them what we'd done to Sam. But I felt awful. I knew what we were doing was mean. But I did it anyway."

Marny is twenty now and in college. But she still thinks about that night and feels guilty.

"I'm usually a nice person," she says. "But I was a different girl that night. I can't blame my friends; they didn't make me do it. I just went right along. I did something I knew was wrong."[1]

Peer Pressure

Psychologists, people who study human behavior, know that people behave differently in groups than when they are by themselves. The power that friends have over one another is called **peer pressure. Peers** are those people who are the same age or in the same group as you are. When people feel they have to go along with what others are doing just to fit in, that is peer pressure.

Sometimes it is hard to say no to a group of friends. They can be persuasive, as Marny's friends were. Like many young people, Marny agreed to go along with her friends—even though she knew it was wrong.

Peer pressure is powerful because of people's need to be liked and accepted.

Marny knows that she would not have called Sam on her own. She felt the need to go along with what Julie and Sarah wanted to do. That is why she called Sam—even though she knew it was mean. This is because the need to be liked by peers is often stronger than good judgment.

Greg, fifteen, admits that peer pressure clouded his judgment. When he was thirteen, he was with some friends who were drinking wine in a nearby park. Greg had never been tempted to drink alcohol. He knew it was wrong because he was under the legal drinking age.

When teenagers try to impress their friends by drinking and driving, it can lead to tragedy.

"But my friends were like, 'Hey, Greg, come on,' and 'You'll like it,'" he says. "I didn't want to look stupid. So I had some wine—which I pretended to like. The bad part was that the more we drank, the louder we got. Somebody must have complained about the noise, because two policemen came and took us to the station. Our parents had to come get us. I was grounded for a month—no phone, no TV, nothing."[2]

Not Always Easy to See

The peer pressure that Greg and Marny felt was obvious. In both cases, their friends persuaded them to do something, even though both knew it was not a good idea. But people can feel peer pressure even when their friends do not try to persuade them. In cases like this, the pressure is not always as obvious.

Janie felt this type of peer pressure. She is a talented athlete who has played soccer since she was five. Even though she is in just the sixth grade, the coach of the ninth grade team has praised her. The coach told Janie she is good enough to play on the high school team.

But the peer pressure Janie feels is not from soccer players. It is from the girls in her grade, and it happens at lunchtime.

"I try to eat well," says Janie. "I burn a lot of calories, so I need to eat enough to give me energy for soccer practice. But my friends in school don't eat much for lunch. Lots of times they don't eat anything at all. Or they'll have an apple or a couple of carrot sticks.

"When I sit down with them, they look at my tray. Sometimes they say things like, 'Janie, you eat like a guy.' Or sometimes they don't say anything, but they kind of raise their eyebrows, you know? It's like, 'How can you eat all that?'"

Eating Like the Girls

Janie says that she feels embarrassed. She does not want to be compared to a boy. She wants her friends to like her, and to feel as though she is one of them. Even though they never tried to persuade her to eat the same way they do, she feels pressure.

"I've stopped eating the regular lunches," she admits. "I usually have what most of them have— carrot sticks or just a little salad."

But Janie says she is not happy about it. "I'm hungry all the time, and I get kind of light-headed

Athletes need to eat more than their peers and should resist the pressure to diet.

A group of friends shares conversation and a meal.

during practice," she says. "I know it's my fault—no one told me to eat like a rabbit at lunch. I decided to do it all on my own. But I hate myself for being so weak. Why do I care if [my friends] raise their eyebrows at what I eat for lunch?"[3]

How can a person allow friends to have so much influence? Psychologists know that peer pressure is not something a person can avoid. In fact, it is actually a normal part of everyone's life.

11

Chapter Two

The Growing Importance of Peers

A **peer group** is not important early in a child's life. Very young children do not worry about fitting in with a group of friends. What other young children say or do has little influence. Instead, parents are the biggest influence early in life. What parents say and how they act have a big effect on their children. That is why being a parent is such an important responsibility.

From Home to Peer Group

Part of a parent's job is to help the child learn important lessons—from telling the truth to not playing with matches. But another important **role** is meeting the child's **emotional** needs. The need to feel wanted and included is as important to young children as it is when they become young adults. When they are little, the parents make sure their children feel that way.

"Everyone enjoys feeling wanted," says one counselor. "Of course, for young children, parents fill that role. When mom or dad smiles and hugs you after school, it feels good. When we are little, that's enough."[4]

As children grow, however, their world expands. Their environment is not only the family, but it also includes classmates and friends. As they get older, children find it fun to be in a group of other children. Friendship and the support of peers becomes more important than it was before.

The smile of her mother is enough to make this young girl feel wanted.

If Peer Groups Did Not Exist

Some might argue that this need to belong and feel important creates trouble. As peers become more important, peer pressure can create problems. Children spend less time with their families. They may get into trouble by experimenting with smoking and drinking because their friends urge them to. What if the peer group did not play as big a role? What if children and teens spent more time at home with family, and less time with peers?

As children grow, the need to interact with peers becomes very important.

Experiments have shown that being raised isolated from peers creates problems. Scientists did studies on monkeys because young monkeys behave a lot like human children. Under normal conditions, young monkeys spend time with their mothers as well as play with each another. In one study, scientists kept some very young monkeys away from one another. This group of monkeys spent all their time with only their mothers. Meanwhile, the normal monkeys spent time with their mothers but had lots of time to play with one another, too.

After a year, the experimenal monkeys were allowed to play with the normally raised monkey. But when they were released, the experimental monkeys did not know how to play with other monkeys. They had a hard time getting along with their peers. Some even preferred being alone.

Psychologists believe there are strong similarities with human children. They say a balance is best. To grow up healthy, children need to have loving parents *and* a peer group. As children grow, a peer group is very important.

The Benefits of Peers

A child's peer group does have some benefits—especially in childhood. For example, it allows children to challenge themselves against people their own age. A seven-year-old girl whose father has taught her to play checkers can see how good she is when she plays against a friend. It is not the same as playing with a parent.

"It's not the same when you play games with your parents," says Maddie, age ten. "They usually let you win. That's fun for a little while, but it gets boring when you figure out that they're just pretending to lose. You know they could beat you if they tried."[5]

Another benefit of a child's peer group is the healthy control it can have. Children do not usually want to act in ways that will make their friends angry. A little boy who is being selfish, for instance, may listen to friends who criticize him for being that way.

"I think lots of parents know how that works," says one mother. "The first day you hear some little kids scolding someone for not sharing toys, or for being too rough, or something. As a parent, you think, 'Hey, they listen to each other more than to me!'"[6]

Positive Control, Too

A peer group's control does more than just solve behavioral problems. Other children's praise is as valuable as their criticism—maybe more so. Of course, parents often praise their children's accomplishments. But by a certain age, that praise is not as important as praise from peers.

"My mom always told me I had a good imagination," says one girl. "Every time I wrote a story in school, she'd save it in a scrapbook. She and my dad thought I should be a writer when I grew up. But it's like anything else—your parents say things because they love you. I felt like I could have written anything and they'd like it.

"But in fifth grade, we had to write a story and read it out loud. When I read mine, some of the kids applauded. And they weren't even really friends of mine! They told me it was the best story of all of them. That made me feel really good. And like I said, they didn't have to say anything—but they did. It was better than my parents telling me

This young student turns to a peer for evaluation of her work.

for the millionth time I was a good writer. This time, I believed it!"[7]

"Sometimes I Didn't Feel Like Me"

By the time a child is about eleven, the peer group becomes far more important than before. This is when **adolescence** begins, the long process of becoming

Adolescence can be a time of confusion and frustration.

an adult. Adolescence lasts about nine years, but it can seem like longer to both the adolescent and the parent.

The changes are gradual. The adolescent's body becomes more like an adult's. There are emotional changes, too. At one moment a thirteen-year-old girl can act very mature, and the next she seems more like a six-year-old child. It is frustrating for teachers and parents. It is even more frustrating—and a bit frightening—for the adolescent.

Donell is fifteen, and he knows how hard adolescence is. He was always fairly quiet. Then around the time he turned fourteen he began losing his temper at home and at school.

"My mom kept saying, 'Where'd the real Donell go?' Like the old Donell, you know? She was thinking I changed so much that I didn't seem like me anymore. Sometimes I didn't feel like me. I felt like she was always yelling at me for stuff. At school, I was having problems, too. I blamed everybody else, and everybody else was blaming me. I felt mad sometimes for no reason, you know? I didn't want to be mad, I just was."[8]

Friends as Allies

Another boy, thirteen, says that neither his parents nor his teachers seem to understand him. "If I have to listen to how easy my life is one more time," he complains, "I'm going to lose it. My parents think my biggest problem is studying for a science quiz.

Adolescents often feel that only peers understand the emotional changes they are going through.

They don't know what my life is like. The only people who *do* know are my friends, I think."[9]

Many changes occur during adolescence. These changes are new and difficult. Adolescents may face choices, such as whether to try smoking and drinking. Also, activities such as dating, which once seemed

unimportant, become everyday concerns. Even when parents want to help, kids do not always want their help.

"My mom tries, but she doesn't know what it's like," says Kate. "She wants to be as involved as she always was. But I'm different now. I love her, and I know she loves me. But I'm not running to her with my problems like I used to. I'm not a little girl."[10]

Adolescents often feel more comfortable talking with their peers about problems. While such talk can be helpful, it is also true that peer groups can present their own kinds of problems. These problems can actually make life more difficult for the adolescent.

Chapter Three

A Closer Look at Peer Pressure

Even though peer groups can be positive, problems sometimes arise between peer groups and individuals. Sometimes a person may no longer feel comfortable with the same friends as before.

Not connecting with a certain group can be disappointing. Andy, fifteen, wanted to make the basketball team at his school. He and several of his best friends tried out together. But when the list of boys who made the team was posted, Andy's name was not on it. However, his friends had all made the team.

"Not a Good Fit"

Andy felt terrible. Not only did he not make the team, but he also felt like an outsider among his friends. They tried to make him feel better, Andy says, but it did not work.

"They were saying stuff like 'We'll still hang out together,' and things like that," he says. "But we didn't. Most of the guys on the team hang out together. That's natural, because they spend a lot of time together. They practice every night after school, and they have team dinners sometimes. I felt pretty bad for a while. I did end up making the junior team, though, and I made some other friends doing that."[11]

Experts say that moving in and out of groups is common.

"Kids' interests change so much during adolescence," says one counselor. "You may feel like you enjoy one group of friends, but after a while, you

Skateboarders are drawn to others who share their interest.

may not feel as comfortable. Maybe you aren't getting the kind of friendship you need from them. For whatever reason, you and the group are just not a good fit. It's not only okay to move on, it's healthy."[12]

Conformity

Another problem common in peer groups is **conformity**, or the need to be the same as one another. In a strong peer group conformity among the mem-

Adolescents often dress like their friends.

bers is not uncommon. That happens even with younger children, whose groups are sometimes made up of all boys or all girls. It is common to see a group of young boys reject a girl who wants to play with them. Even if she is a good athlete, the boys might be reluctant to play with her.

Among adolescents, similarity within their peer group is more important than ever. The peer groups at this age are not based on being boys or being girls. Sometimes members of a group have shared interests, such as playing on a team together. Sometimes the members have a similar background, such as religion or race.

To be part of a group, an individual might try to act like everyone else. Experts say that is normal. Adolescence is a time for branching out. It is no longer enough to model behavior after parents. Instead, adolescents begin modeling themselves after friends they admire. They imitate clothing styles, haircuts, and even the slang their peers use.

"Who Buys Ripped Jeans?"

Parents often become annoyed by the way adolescents imitate one another. "I have trouble with it," admits the mother of a twelve-year-old girl. "I hate listening to my daughter talk with her friends. She sounds so phony. She uses the same exact words as they do, and even changes the way she laughs."[13]

Another parent agrees. "I'm disappointed that my daughter can't think for herself anymore. She

Teenagers look through racks of shoes for a style both they and their friends will like.

used to. She used to be an individual, with her own opinions. Now, she acts like she can't make a move without permission from her friends."[14]

Such conformity can be expensive, too. Fashions go in and out of style, and clothes that were perfect in April are outdated by July. "I have twin daughters, thirteen years old," says one man. "I bought them each two pairs of jeans they couldn't live without. That was in September. And now, they say the jeans aren't good unless they're ripped. I ask, 'Can you just rip them?' They look at me like I'm from Mars. They say, 'No, you have to buy them ripped.' I don't get it. Who buys ripped jeans?"[15]

More Serious Conformity

But sometimes conformity is more than dressing alike or talking alike. It can sometimes mean that the peer group thinks or behaves the same way. Often this sort of conformity can lead to serious problems.

Andrew was thirteen when he became involved with a gang. He knew most of the boys from his neighborhood. Andrew was not sure if he wanted to join at first. He knew they sold drugs. He had also heard that they robbed a store.

"It wasn't that I needed to be a gangster," says Andrew. "I mostly wanted to hang out with guys I knew. I figured I didn't have to do anything I didn't want to do. If they were doing something I wasn't ready for, I'd just back off."

At first, that is how it worked. Andrew liked being with the group of boys. He even liked wearing the blue and black colors that the gang wore. When several of the boys decided to get tattoos with a gang symbol on their arms, Andrew did that, too.

"I Should Have Stopped"

But conformity had a price. Andrew found that it became hard to say no to the gang. If he did not want to do something that they were doing, they did not like it.

Drinking is one dangerous way that teens conform to the behavior of peer groups.

Street gangs are peer groups whose members conform to violent behavior.

"It seemed easier just to go along," he says. "I didn't want to fight with them, you know? So I'd just say okay, when they wanted to do something."

One night he and four of the other boys were caught breaking into a house. Andrew had not wanted to do it, but he did. Andrew and two other boys were caught.

"It was a really bad time," he says. "We ended up in a detention center, and then we had to go to court. My mom was really upset, really angry with me. She told me I was old enough to know right from wrong. And I was—I know. But it was hard to stop with those guys. I should have stopped, but it was too hard."

Andrew left the gang after his arrest. His mother and his social worker made sure he used his time better. He did work at his church, and worked a part-time job. Andrew knows he is lucky.

"If I'd stayed in that gang, I would have done worse things," he says. "Now things are better. I don't feel like I'm being pushed into stuff I don't like."[16]

Chapter Four

Being an Individual

Many young people complain that adults do not understand them. They say that parents and teachers do not realize how strong peer pressure can be.

"My mom is always saying, 'Be your own person,' like that's easy," says Donell. "But she doesn't know what it's like. When she was a teenager, things were different. Kids didn't have the same problems then. I wish she wouldn't make it sound like it's so simple not to care about what other people think."[17]

A Strong Force

Psychologists know that peer pressure is very strong. After all, it can often make people ignore common sense. But how strong a force is peer pressure? Psychologists did an experiment to see if a peer group could force someone to doubt what he or she actually saw or heard. The psychologists were surprised by the results.

In the experiment, psychologists brought five fourth-graders into a room. They told the kids they were going to play a game. The kids were shown twelve cards, each with two lines printed on them. They were supposed to look at the lines, and say which they thought was longer—line A or line B.

Peer pressure can make it very difficult to behave as an individual.

Class participation may be influenced by peer pressure.

A Trick

The game sounded easy but there was a trick. The psychologists had secretly talked to four of the five students ahead of time. The four were told to say the wrong answer on purpose. The fifth was not told of the trick. The fifth was placed at the end of the row and always answered last.

Time after time the experiment was done. And each time, the results were almost the same. The

to try to be like everyone else. For adolescents, it is much harder. Keeping peer pressure under control seems impossible sometimes.

Experts say that the difficulties of adolescent peer pressure do not last. By age fifteen or sixteen, the worst is usually over. By that age, teens are usually stronger and more confident. They are not as likely to do something dangerous or foolish just to be liked.

Having the strength to control peer pressure comes from many sources. Sometimes it helps to talk to a teacher, a counselor, or another trusted adult. Marah, thirteen, found that she was stronger after talking to her grandmother.

"She's really special," says Marah. "I can tell her things, and she doesn't judge me. But she tells me stories about how she would handle problems when she was a girl. She had guts, too! So when I feel pressured to do something, I think about her. I say to myself, 'What would Grandma do now?' And it doesn't take long to find the right answer."[20]

Making Changes

Sometimes peer pressure can be so intense, that every day is a new challenge. When that happens, say experts, it is good to make some changes. For Luis, his peer group was wrong for him. He thought he wanted to be in that group at first, but he later changed his mind.

"I learned the hard way," he says. "I got in trouble for helping my friend Edgar cheat on a paper. I

Talking to a trusted adult is a great way to keep peer pressure under control.

am good in English, but Edgar wasn't. All our friends said, 'Luis, write a paper for him.' I knew I shouldn't. I told them if we got caught, we'd flunk. But Edgar was desperate. He said, 'Come on, man, if you don't help me, I'll fail English.' So I wrote him a paper.

"But the teacher figured it out. We both got Fs on that paper—even though mine was really an A. Also, we both got twenty hours of detention for cheating. I was mad at Edgar at first. But then I was mad at myself. I'm not hanging around with Edgar and those guys. I don't get anything from them but trouble."[21]

Choosing a positive peer group can make the difficulties of adolescence easier to cope with.

Learning to handle pressure from friends can contribute to self-confidence.

Luis's teacher helped him make some changes, too. She asked him to be part of the school newspaper staff. He is busy after school four days a week. He has become more confident because he is doing a good job. As a result of this new confidence, he does not give in to peer pressure as easily. He has made some new friends, too.

Good Choices

Marny says that learning to handle peer pressure was hard. She made mistakes along the way. But eventually, she learned that she did not need her friends to tell her what to do. She was able to make choices by herself.

"That's the best thing," she says. "The first time you say 'No, I don't feel like doing that,' when your friends want to do something you know is stupid—it's great. You feel strong, and it's even easier the second time. Every time you make a good decision, you are closer to being an adult."[22]

Notes

Chapter One: The Power of the Peer Group

1. Personal interview, Marny, June 15, 2002, Minneapolis.
2. Personal interview, Greg, February 17–18, 1996, Columbia Heights, Minnesota.
3. Personal interview, Janie, June 19, 2002, Richfield, Minnesota.

Chapter Two: The Growing Importance of Peers

4. Telephone interview, Lynne, July 5, 2002.
5. Personal interview, Maddie, July 19, 2002, Blaine, Minnesota.
6. Telephone interview, Terry, July 12, 2002.
7. Personal interview, Kate H., July 6, 2002, Richfield.
8. Personal interview, Donell, March 20–21, 1996, Minneapolis.
9. Personal interview, [name withheld], August 1999, St. Paul, Minnesota.
10. Telephone interview, Kate B., July 22, 2002.

Chapter Three: A Closer Look at Peer Pressure

11. Personal interview, Andy S., September 1997.
12. Interview, Lynne.
13. Telephone interview, Jane, July 16, 2002.
14. Personal interview, Gillian, June 30, 2002, Minneapolis.
15. Personal interview, Joe, June 30, 2002, Minneapolis.

16. Personal interview, Andrew, March 1996, Minneapolis.

Chapter Four: Being an Individual

17. Interview, Donell.

18. Telephone interview, Joe, July 13, 2002.

19. Personal interview, Esther, June 12, 2002, Bloomington, Minnesota.

20. Personal interview, Marah, August 12, 1999, St. Paul.

21. Personal interview, Luis, September 2000, Stillwater, Minnesota.

22. Interview, Marny.

Glossary

adolescence: The stage in life between being a child and being an adult.

conformity: Trying to be like everyone else.

emotional: Having to do with feelings.

peer: A friend or a classmate.

peer group: A group of friends or classmates who have certain interests in common.

peer pressure: The influential power friends have over one another.

psychologists: People who study human behavior.

role: A job or function that a person may perform in a family or group.

For Further Exploration

Robyn M. Feller, *Everything You Need to Know About Peer Pressure*. New York: Rosen Publishing, 2001. Slightly more difficult reading, but a good section on making decisions.

Gershen Kaufman, Lev Raphael, and Pamela Espeland, *Stick Up for Yourself: Every Kid's Guide to Personal Power and Positive Self-Esteem*. Minneapolis: Free Spirit Publishing, 1999. Good information on being an individual in tough situations.

Trevor Romain, *Cliques, Phonies, and Other Baloney*. Minneapolis: Free Spirit Publishing, 1998. Well written and funny. Very good information on being rejected by a peer group.

Index

Picture Credits

About the Author

Gail B. Stewart has written over ninety books for young people, including a series for Lucent Books called The Other America. She has written many books on historical topics such as World War I and the Warsaw ghetto.

Stewart received her undergraduate degree from Gustavus Adolphus College in St. Peter, Minnesota. She did her graduate work in English, linguistics, and curriculum study at the University of St. Thomas and the University of Minnesota. She taught English and reading for more than ten years. Stewart and her husband live in Minneapolis with their three sons.